Jana Hauschild

FLORAL CHARTED DESIGNS

Dover Publications, Inc.
NEW YORK

Published in Canada by General Publishing Company, Ltd., 30 Lesmill Road, Don Mills, Toronto, Ontario.

Published in the United Kingdom by Constable and Company, Ltd., 10 Orange Street, London WC2H 7EG.

Floral Charted Designs is a new work, first published by Dover Publications, Inc., in 1984.

Manufactured in the United States of America
Dover Publications, Inc., 31 East 2nd Street, Mineola, N.Y. 11501

Library of Congress Cataloging in Publication Data

Lindberg, Jana Hauschild.
Floral charted designs.

(Dover needlework series)
1. Needlework—Patterns. 2. Decoration and ornament—Plant forms. I. Title. II. Series.
TT753.L54 1984 746.44′041 83-6221
ISBN 0-486-24750-3

INTRODUCTION

With several very successful books to her credit, Jana Hauschild, long one of the foremost European designers, now needs no introduction to American needleworkers. Featured in this new collection are some of her loveliest floral designs in a wide variety of sizes and formats: square and circular borders, small motifs, overall patterns and some particularly stunning large-scale creations that can be used to make wall hangings of heirloom quality.

All of the designs are charted for ready use in different forms of needlework such as counted cross-stitch, needlepoint, latch-hooking, crochet and knitting. To give inspiration, all of the designs are shown on the covers as completed projects. You can make the items shown or use the charts to create your own needlework designs. The possibilities are as wonderful as they are endless!

Keep in mind that the finished piece of needlework will not be the same size as the charted design unless you happen to be working on fabric (or canvas) that has the same number of threads per inch as the chart has squares per inch. With knitting and crocheting, the size will vary according to the number of stitches per inch.

To determine how large a finished counted cross-stitch design will be, divide the number of stitches in the design by the thread-count of the fabric. For example, if a design that is 112 stitches wide by 140 stitches deep is worked on a 14-count cloth, divide 112 stitches by 14 to get 8 and 140 by 14 to get 10; so the worked design will measure 8″ × 10″. The same design worked on 22-count fabric would measure approximately 5″ × 6½″.

Most of these designs were originally created for counted cross-stitch; one of the great advantages to this craft is that the supplies and equipment required are minimal and inexpensive. You will need:

1. A small blunt tapestry needle, #24 or #26.
2. Evenweave fabric. This can be linen, cotton, wool or a blend that includes miracle fibers. The three most popular fabrics are:

Cotton Aida. This is made 14 threads per inch, 11 threads per inch, 8 threads per inch, and so forth. Fourteen, being the prettiest, is preferred.

Evenweave Linen. This also comes in a variety of threads per inch. Working on evenweave linen involves a slightly different technique, which is explained on page 5. Thirty-count linen will give a stitch approximately the same size as 14-count aida.

Hardanger Cloth. This has 22 threads per inch and is available in cotton or linen.

3. Embroidery thread. This can be six-strand mercerized cotton floss (DMC, Coats and Clark, Lily, Anchor, etc.), crewel wool, Danish Flower Thread, silken and metal threads or pearl cotton. DMC embroidery thread has been used to color-code all of the patterns in this book. One skein of each color given in the color key is needed, unless otherwise indicated in parentheses. For 14-count aida and 30-count linen, divide six-strand cotton floss and work with only two strands. For more texture, use more thread; for a flatter look, use less thread. Crewel wool is pretty on an evenweave wool fabric, and some embroiderers even use wool on cotton fabric. Danish Flower Thread is a thicker thread with a matte finish, one strand equaling two of cotton floss.
4. Embroidery hoop. Use a plastic or wooden 4″, 5″ or 6″ round or oval hoop with a screw type tension adjuster.
5. A pair of sharp embroidery scissors is absolutely essential.

Prepare the fabric by whipping, hemming or zigzagging on the sewing machine to prevent raveling at the edges. Next, locate the exact center of the design you have chosen, so that you can then center the design on the piece of fabric. Many of the designs in the book have an arrow at the top and along one side; follow the indicated rows to where they intersect; this is the center stitch. Next, find the center of the fabric by folding it in half both vertically and horizontally. The center stitch of the design should fall where the creases in the fabric meet.

It's usually not very convenient to begin work with the center stitch itself. As a rule it's better to start at the top of a design, working horizontal rows of a single color, left to right. This technique permits you to go from an unoccupied space to an occupied space (from an empty hole to a filled one), which makes ruffling the floss less likely. To find out where the top of the design should be placed, count squares up from the center of the design, and then count off the corresponding number of holes up from the center of the fabric.

Next, place the section of the fabric to be worked tautly in the hoop; the tighter the better, for tension makes it easier to push the needle through the holes without piercing the fabric. As you work, use the screw adjuster to tighten as necessary. Keep the screw at the top and out of your way.

Counted cross-stitch is very simple. When beginning, fasten thread with a waste knot by holding a bit of thread on the underside of the work and anchoring it with the first few stitches *(diagram 1)*. To stitch, push the threaded needle up

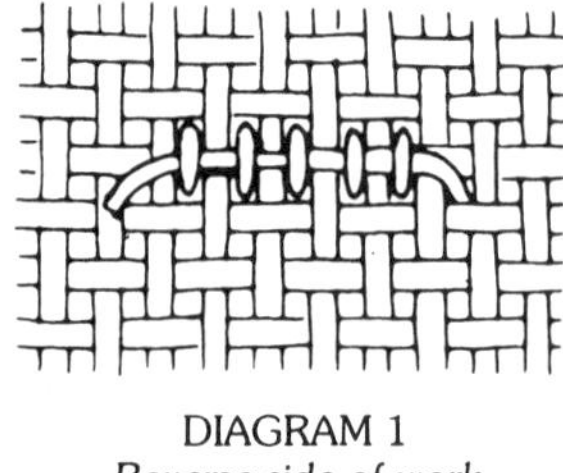

DIAGRAM 1
Reverse side of work

through a hole in the fabric and cross over the thread intersection (or square) diagonally, left to right *(diagram 2)*. This is half the stitch. Now cross back, right to left, making an X *(diagram 3)*. Do all the stitches in the same color in the same row, working left to right and slanting from bottom left to upper

DIAGRAM 2

right *(diagram 3)*. Then cross back, completing the X's *(diagram 4)*. Some cross-stitchers prefer to cross each stitch as they come to it; this is fine, but be sure the slant is always in the correct direction. Of course, isolated stitches must be crossed as you work them. Vertical stitches are crossed as shown in

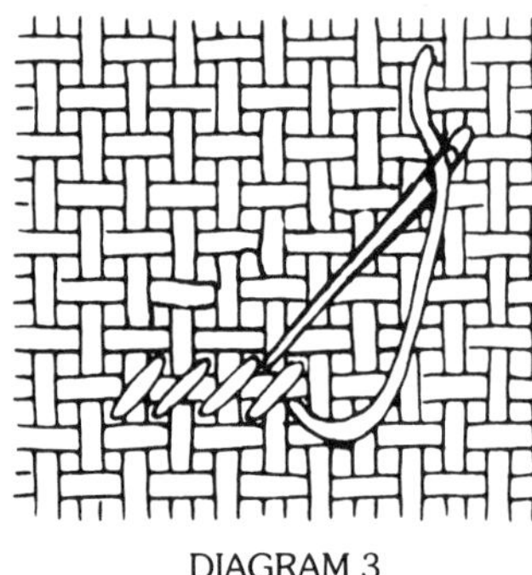

DIAGRAM 3

DIAGRAM 4

diagram 5. Holes are used more than once; all stitches "hold hands" unless a space is indicated. The work is always held upright, never turned as for some needlepoint stitches.

When carrying a color from one area to another, wiggle your needle under existing stitches on the underside. Do not carry a color across an open expanse of fabric for more than a few stitches, as the thread will be visible from the front. Remember, in counted cross-stitch you do not work the background.

DIAGRAM 5

To end a color, weave in and out of the underside of stitches, perhaps making a scallop stitch or two for extra security *(diagram 6)*. Whenever possible, end in the direction in which you are traveling, jumping up a row if necessary *(diagram 7)*. This prevents holes caused by work being pulled in two directions. Do not make knots; knots make bumps. Cut off the ends of the threads; do not leave any tails because they'll show through when the work is mounted.

Another stitch used in counted cross-stitch is the backstitch. This is worked from hole to hole and may be vertical, horizontal or slanted *(diagram 8)*.

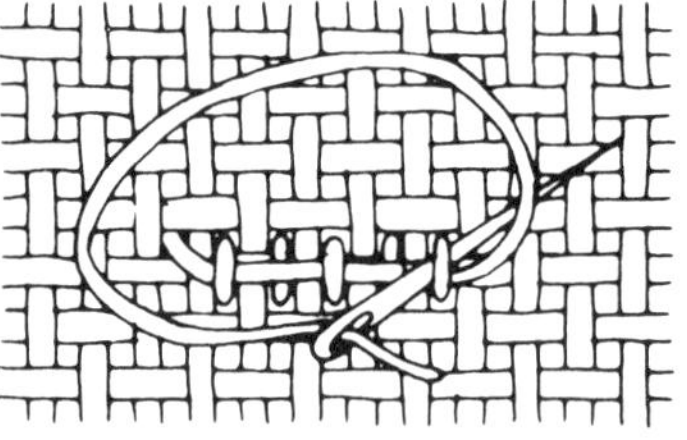

DIAGRAM 6
Reverse side of work

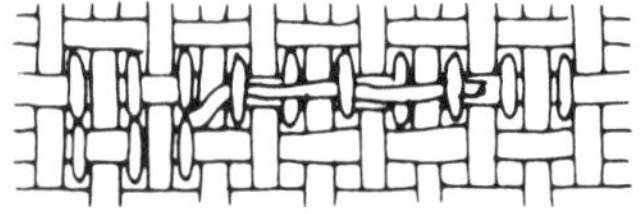

DIAGRAM 7
Reverse side of work

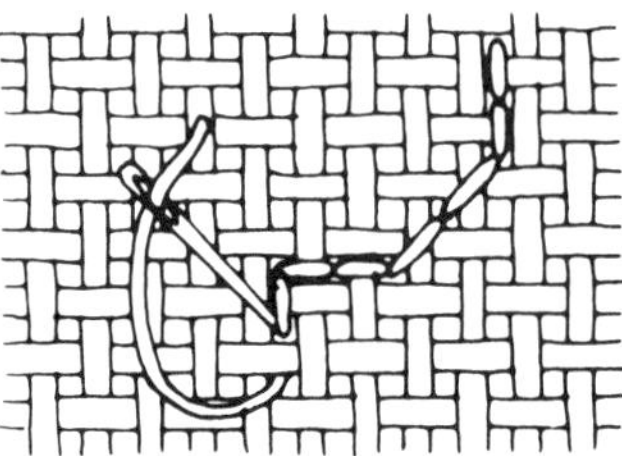

DIAGRAM 8

Working on linen requires a slightly different technique. Evenweave linen is remarkably regular, but there are always some thin threads and some that are nubbier or fatter than others. To even these out and to make a stitch that is easy to see, the cross-stitch is worked over two threads each way. The "square" you are covering is thus 4 threads *(diagram 9)*. The first few stitches on linen are sometimes difficult, but one quickly begins "to see in twos." After the third stitch, a pattern is established, and should you inadvertently cross over three threads instead of four, the difference in slant will make it immediately apparent that you have erred.

Linen evenweave fabric should be worked with the selvage at the side, not at the top and bottom.

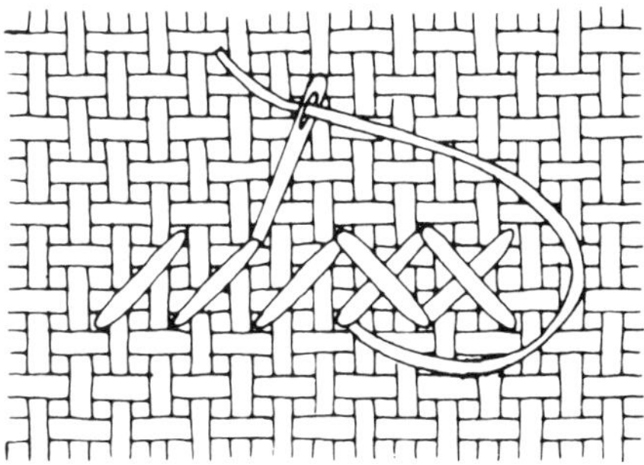

DIAGRAM 9

Because you go over more threads, linen affords more variations in stitches. A half stitch can slant in either direction and is uncrossed. A three-fourths stitch is shown in *diagram 10*. *Diagram 11* shows backstitch on linen.

DIAGRAM 10

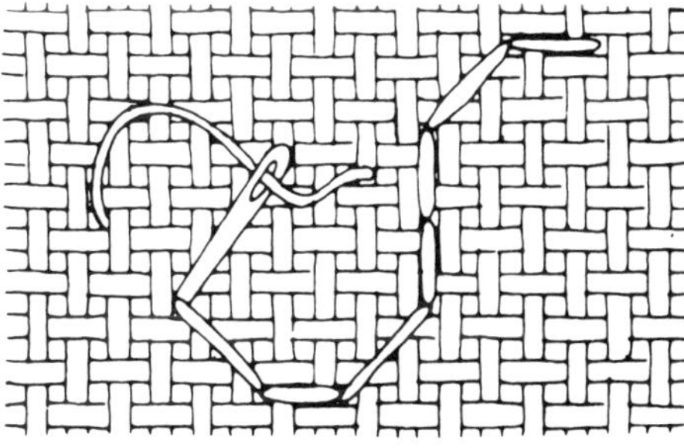

DIAGRAM 11

Gingham or other checkered material can also be used for counted cross-stitch by making the crosses over the checks from corner to corner. If you wish to embroider a cross-stitch design onto a fabric that does not have an even weave, baste a lightweight Penelope canvas to the fabric. The design can then be worked from the chart by making crosses over the double mesh of the canvas, being careful not to catch the threads of the canvas in the sewing. When the design is completed, the basting stitches are removed, and the horizontal and then the vertical threads of the canvas are removed, one strand at a time, with a tweezers. The cross-stitch design will remain on the fabric.

After you have completed your embroidery, wash it in cool or lukewarm water with a mild soap. Rinse well. Do not wring. Roll in a towel to remove excess moisture. Immediately iron on a padded surface with the embroidery face down. Be sure the embroidery is completely dry before attempting to mount it.

To mount as a picture, center the embroidery over a pure white, rag-content mat board. Turn margins over to the back evenly. Lace the margins with sturdy thread, top to bottom, side to side. The fabric should be tight and even, with a little tension. Never use glue for mounting. Counted cross-stitch on cotton or linen may be framed under glass. Wool needs to breathe and should not be framed under glass unless a breathing space is left.

Charted designs can also be used for needlepoint. The designs can be worked directly onto needlepoint canvas by counting off the correct number of warp and weft squares shown on the chart, each square representing one stitch to be taken on the canvas. If you prefer to put some guidelines on the canvas, make certain that your marking medium is waterproof. Use either nonsoluble inks, acrylic paints thinned appropriately with water so as not to clog the holes in the canvas, or oil paints mixed with benzine or turpentine. Felt-tipped pens are very handy, but check the labels carefully because not all felt markers are waterproof. It is a good idea to experiment with any writing materials on a piece of scrap canvas to make certain that all material is waterproof. There is nothing worse than having a bit of ink run onto the needlepoint as you are blocking it.

There are two distinct types of needlepoint canvas: single-mesh and double-mesh. Double-mesh is woven with two horizontal and two vertical threads forming each mesh, whereas single-mesh is woven with one vertical and one horizontal thread forming each mesh. Double-mesh is a very stable canvas on which the threads will stay securely in place as you work. Single-mesh canvas, which is more widely used, is a little easier on the eyes because the spaces are slightly larger.

A tapestry needle with a rounded, blunt tip and an elongated eye is used for needlepoint. The most commonly used needle for #10 canvas is the #18 needle. The needle should clear the hole in the canvas without spreading the threads. Special yarns that have good twist and are sufficiently heavy to cover the canvas are used for needlepoint.

Although there are over a hundred different needlepoint stitches, the Tent Stitch is universally considered to be *the* needlepoint stitch. The three most familiar versions of Tent Stitch are: Plain Half-Cross Stitch, Continental Stitch and Basket Weave Stitch.

Plain Half-Cross Stitch *(diagram 12)*. Always work Half-Cross Stitch from left to right, then turn the canvas around and work the return row, still stitching from left to right. Bring the needle to the front of the canvas at a point that will be the bottom of the first stitch. The needle is in a vertical position when making the stitch. Keep the stitches loose for minimum distortion and good coverage. This stitch must be worked on a double-mesh canvas.

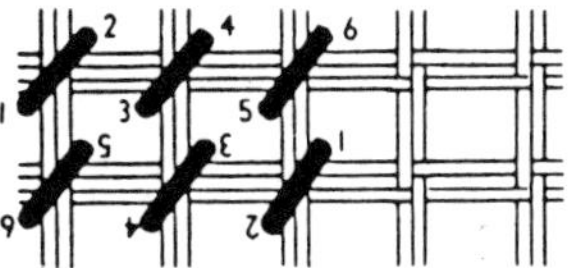

DIAGRAM 12

Continental Stitch *(diagram 13).* Start this design at the upper right-hand corner and work from right to left. The needle is slanted and always brought out a mesh ahead. The resulting stitch is actually a Half-Cross Stitch on top and a slanting stitch on the back. When the row is finished, turn the canvas around and work the return row, still stitching from right to left.

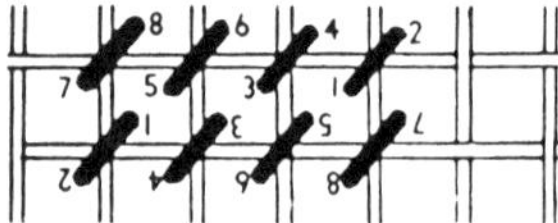

DIAGRAM 13

Basket Weave Stitch *(diagram 14).* Start in the upper right-hand corner of the area with four Continental Stitches, two worked horizontally across the top and two placed directly below the first stitch. Then work diagonal rows, the first slanting up and across the canvas from right to left and the next down and across from left to right. Each new row is one stitch longer. As you go down the canvas (left to right), the needle is held in a vertical position; as you move in the opposite direction, the needle is horizontal. The rows should interlock, creating a basket-weave pattern on the reverse. If this is not done properly, a faint ridge will show where the pattern was interrupted. Always stop working in the middle of a row, rather than at the end, so that you will know in which direction you were working.

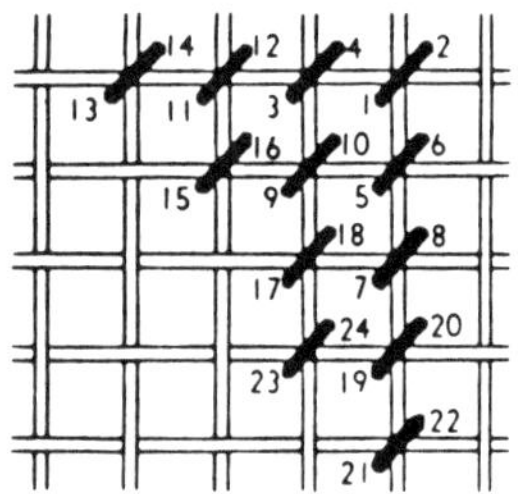

DIAGRAM 14

Bind all the raw edges of needlepoint canvas with masking tape, double-fold bias tape or even adhesive tape. There are no set rules on where to begin a design. Generally it is easier to begin close to the center and work outward toward the edges of the canvas, working the backgrounds or borders last. To avoid fraying the yarn, work with strands not longer than 18″.

When you have finished your needlepoint, it should be blocked. No matter how straight you have kept your work, blocking will give it a professional look.

Any hard, flat surface that you do not mind marring with nail holes and one that will not be warped by wet needlepoint can serve as a blocking board. A large piece of plywood, an old drawing board or an old-fashioned doily blocker are ideal.

Moisten a Turkish towel in cold water and roll the needlepoint in the towel. Leaving the needlepoint in the towel overnight will insure that both the canvas and the yarn are thoroughly and evenly dampened. Do not saturate the needlepoint! Never hold the needlepoint under the faucet as that much water is not necessary.

Mark the desired outline on the blocking board, making sure that the corners are straight. Lay the needlepoint on the blocking board, and tack the canvas with thumbtacks spaced about ½″ to ¾″ apart. It will probably take a good deal of pulling and tugging to get the needlepoint straight, but do not be afraid of this stress. Leave the canvas on the blocking board until thoroughly dry. Never put an iron on your needlepoint. You cannot successfully block with a steam iron because the needlepoint must dry in the straightened position. You may also have needlepoint blocked professionally. If you have a pillow made, a picture framed or a chair seat mounted, the craftsman may include the blocking in the price.

Charted designs can be worked in duplicate stitch over the squares formed by stockinette stitch in knitting or afghan stitch in crochet. The patterns can also be knitted directly into the work by working with more than one color, as in Fair Isle knitting. The wool not in use is always stranded across the back of the work. When it has to be stranded over more than five stitches, it should be twisted around the wool in use on every third stitch, thus preventing long strands at the back of the work. When several colors are used, a method known as "motif knitting" is employed. In this method short lengths of wool are cut and wound on bobbins, using a separate bobbin for each color and twisting the colors where they meet to avoid gaps in the work, as in knitting argyle socks.

CHRISTMAS ROSES

(See color illustration on inside front cover.)

	DMC #			DMC #	
⊡	3045	dark yellow beige		580	dark moss green
⊞	3047	light yellow beige		581	moss green
·	746	off white		221	dark shell pink
	830	medium avocado leaf		3350	very dark dusty rose
⊠	831	light avocado leaf		961	dark dusty rose
	732	olive green		3687	mauve
	734	light olive green		3688	medium mauve

WALL HANGING WITH DANDELIONS

(See color illustration on inside back cover.)

Symbol	DMC #	Color
◣	3345	dark hunter green
◢	3346	hunter green
☒	3347	medium yellow green
◫	471	very light avocado green
●	580	dark moss green
Λ	581	moss green
C	734	light olive green
K	3064	spice
⧅	437	light tan
⊟	3046	medium yellow beige
····⧄	3047	light yellow beige
⊡		snow white
⧅	783	Christmas gold
‖	972	deep canary
L	444	dark lemon
— ■	317	pewter gray
O	793	medium cornflower blue
⁛	794	light cornflower blue

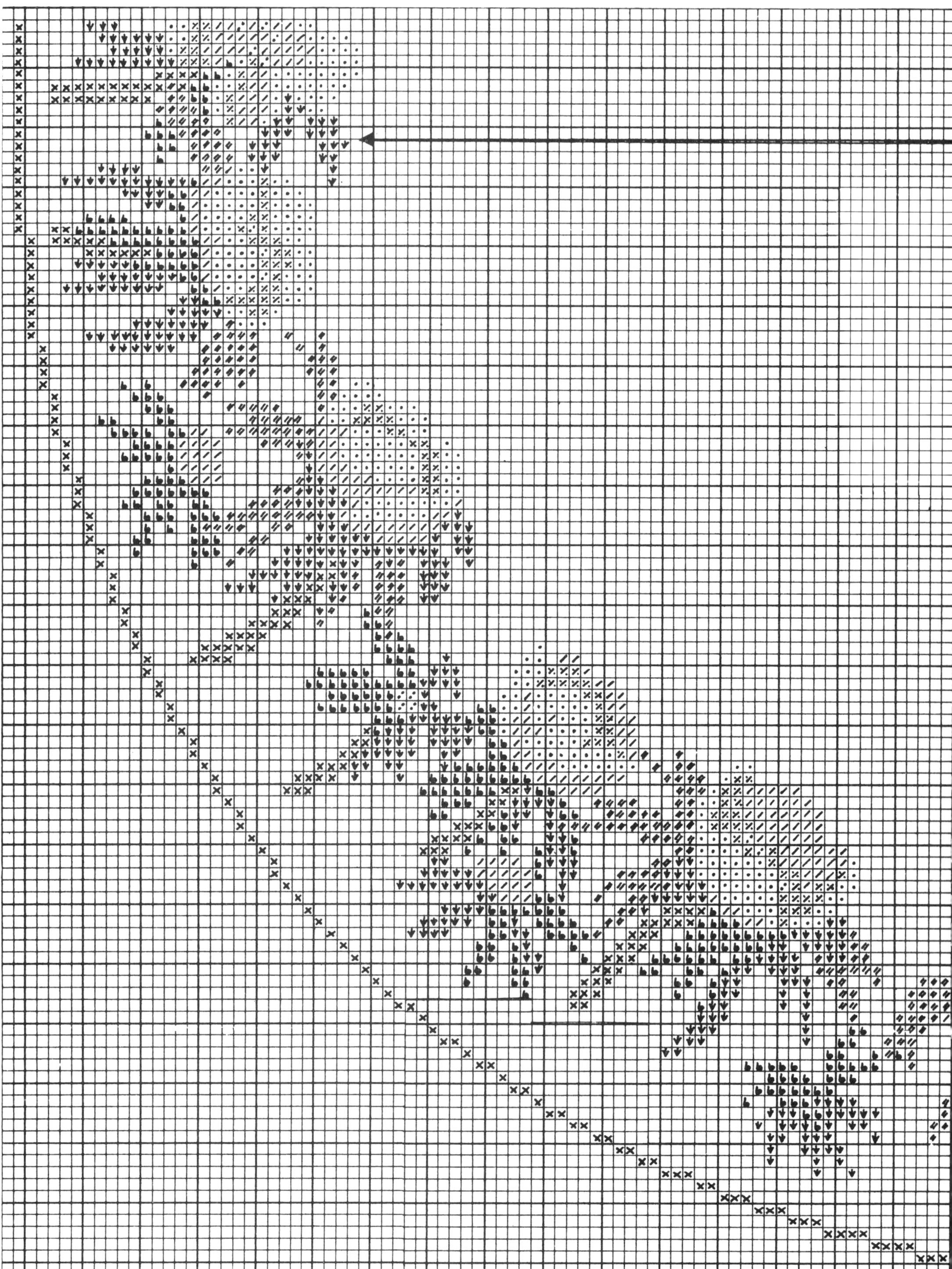

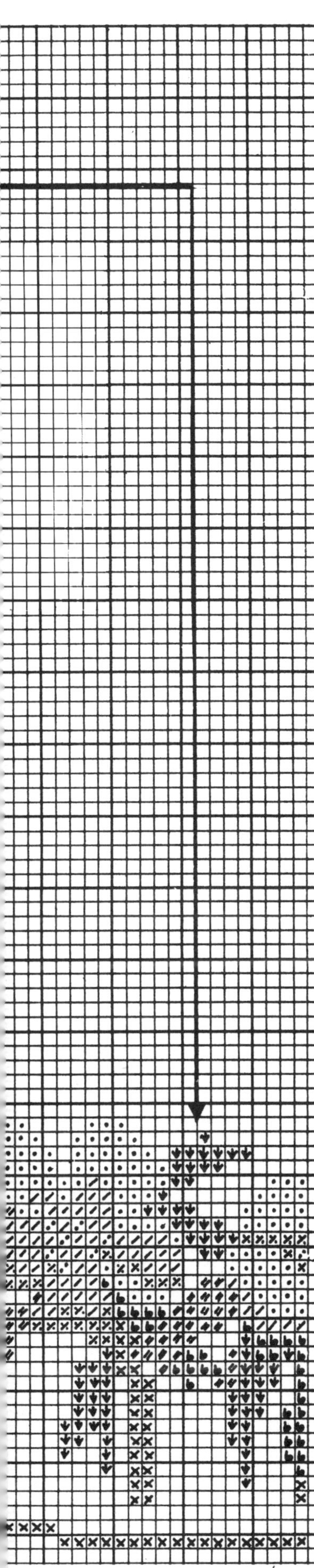

CIRCULAR DESIGN WITH WINTER ACONITE

(See color illustration on back cover.)

	DMC #	
[•]	307	lemon
[/]	444	dark lemon
[⁄.]	742	light tangerine
[.·]	734	light olive green
[X]	832	dark golden wheat
[//]	471	very light avocado green
[↓]	469	avocado green
[b]	3345	dark hunter green

SPRING: APPLE BLOSSOMS

(See color illustration on inside front cover.)

DMC #		DMC #		DMC #	
3021	dark brown gray	3348	light yellow green	818	baby pink
611	dark drab brown	783	Christmas gold	819	light baby pink
3345	dark hunter green	726	light topaz		white
3346	hunter green	893	light carnation		
3347	medium yellow green	776	medium pink		

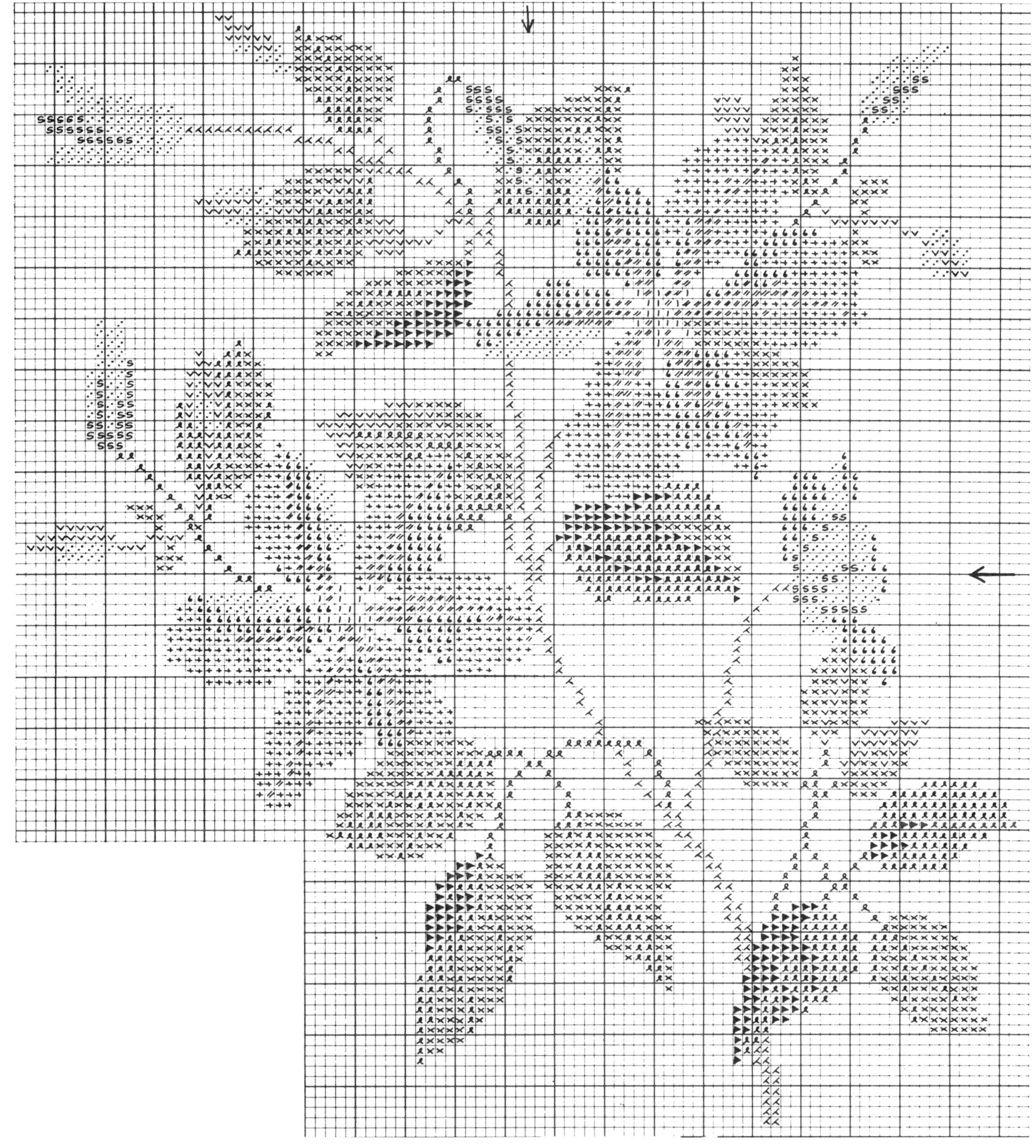

SUMMER: CLEMATIS

(See color illustration on inside front cover.)

	DMC #			DMC #			DMC #	
⊠ (diagonal)	3032	medium mocha brown	V	3348	light yellow green	+	553	medium violet
▶	3345	dark hunter green	ℛ	732	olive green	//	917	medium plum
ℷ	3346	hunter green	I	726	light topaz	S	3041	medium antique violet
⊠	3347	medium yellow green	6	552	dark violet	·	3042	light antique violet

AUTUMN: MOUNTAIN ASH

(See color illustration on inside front cover.)

DMC #		DMC #		DMC #	
3021	dark brown gray	3348	light yellow green	919	red copper
611	dark drab brown	732	olive green	947	burnt orange
3346	hunter green	831	light avocado leaf	349	dark coral
3347	medium yellow green	833	medium golden wheat		

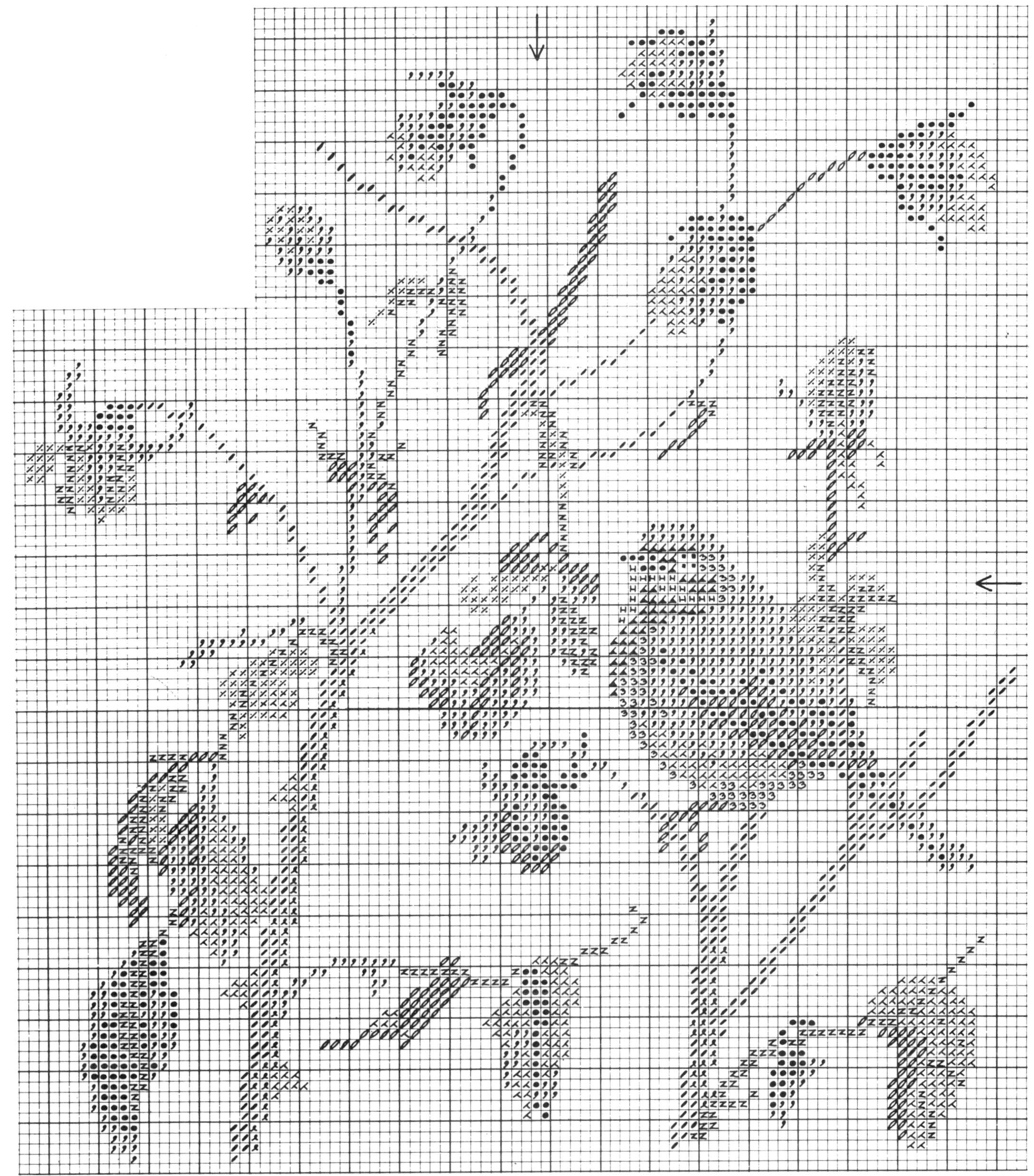

WINTER: ROBIN AND WITHERED ROSES

(See color illustration on inside front cover.)

DMC #		DMC #		DMC #	
3021	dark brown gray	3346	hunter green	414	dark steel gray
839	dark beige brown	831	light avocado leaf	919	red copper
611	dark drab brown	833	medium golden wheat	921	copper
3032	medium mocha brown	310	black	819	light baby pink

MAGNOLIA AND BIRDS WALL HANGING

(See color illustration on inside back cover.)

Symbol	DMC #	Color
●	3346	hunter green
+	3347	medium yellow green
◹	471	very light avocado green
◣	961	dark dusty rose
◸	3688	medium mauve
X	3689	light mauve
L	819	light baby pink
⁚		white
▐	3021	dark brown gray
Λ	610	very dark drab brown
//	3012	medium khaki green
⁚\	3013	light khaki green
N	733	medium olive green
O	834	light golden wheat
—	726	light topaz
K	931	medium antique blue
↑	932	light antique blue
■	310	black

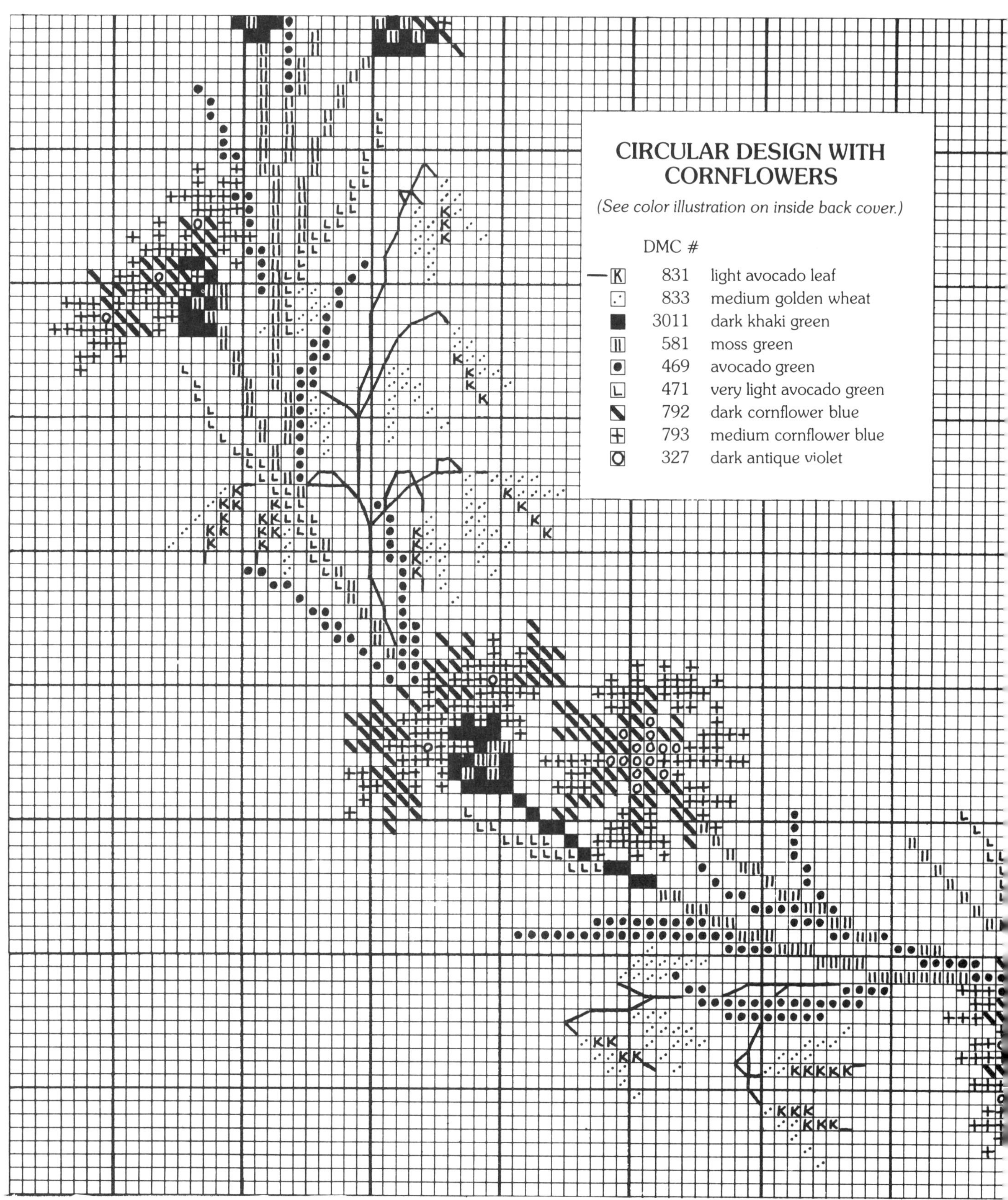

CIRCULAR DESIGN WITH CORNFLOWERS
(See color illustration on inside back cover.)
DMC #
K 831 light avocado leaf
833 medium golden wheat
3011 dark khaki green
581 moss green
469 avocado green
471 very light avocado green
792 dark cornflower blue
793 medium cornflower blue
327 dark antique violet

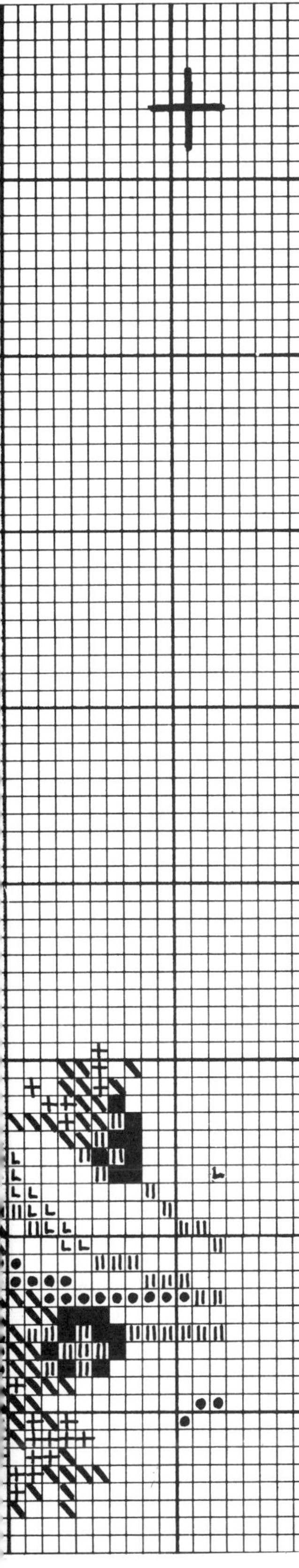

OVERALL PATTERN WITH BLUEBELLS

(See color illustration on inside front cover.)

	DMC #	
—△	729	medium old gold
····■	987	dark forest green
⊞	3347	medium yellow green
☒	793	medium cornflower blue
⎕	794	light cornflower blue
⊡	208	very dark lavender

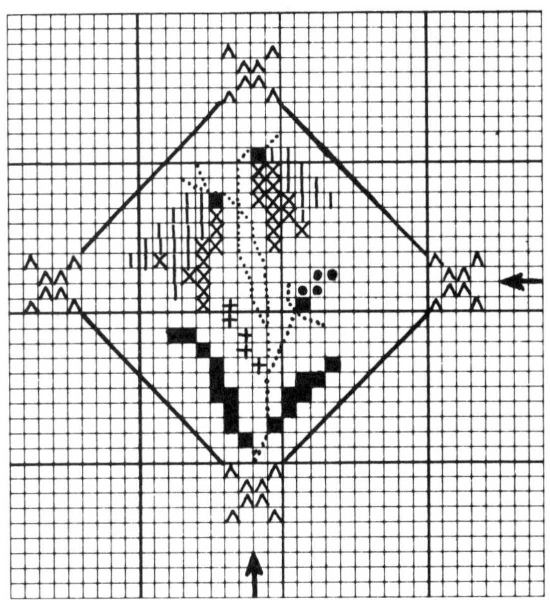

OVERALL PATTERN WITH FORGET-ME-NOTS

(See color illustration on inside front cover.)

	DMC #	
—△	729	medium old gold
····☒	470	light avocado green
⎕	471	very light avocado green
■	208	very dark lavender
ⓞ	209	dark lavender
⧅	554	light violet
⊡	973	bright canary

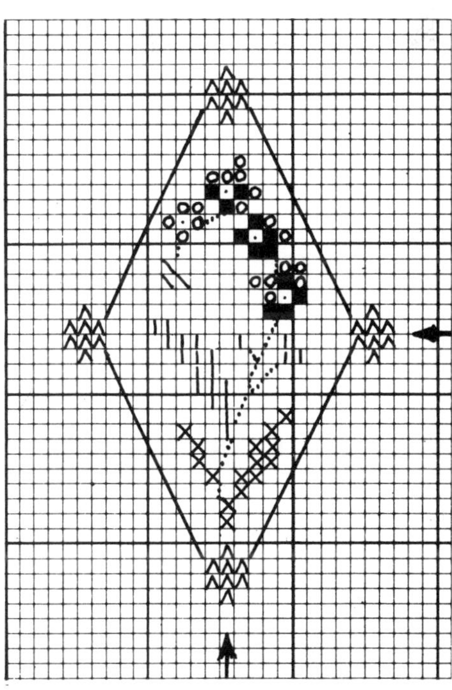

WALL HANGING WITH NASTURTIUMS

(See color illustration on inside back cover.)

Symbol	DMC #	Color	Symbol	DMC #	Color	Symbol	DMC #	Color
◣	986	very dark forest green	⊡ (o)	733	medium olive green	⧅ (\\)	970	light pumpkin
●	987	dark forest green	⊟	734	light olive green	L	741	medium tangerine
Λ	3347	medium yellow green	◢ (/)	919	red copper	·	972	deep canary
I	471	very light avocado green	III	900	dark burnt orange	C	834	light golden wheat
⁘	472	ultra light avocado green	+	947	burnt orange			

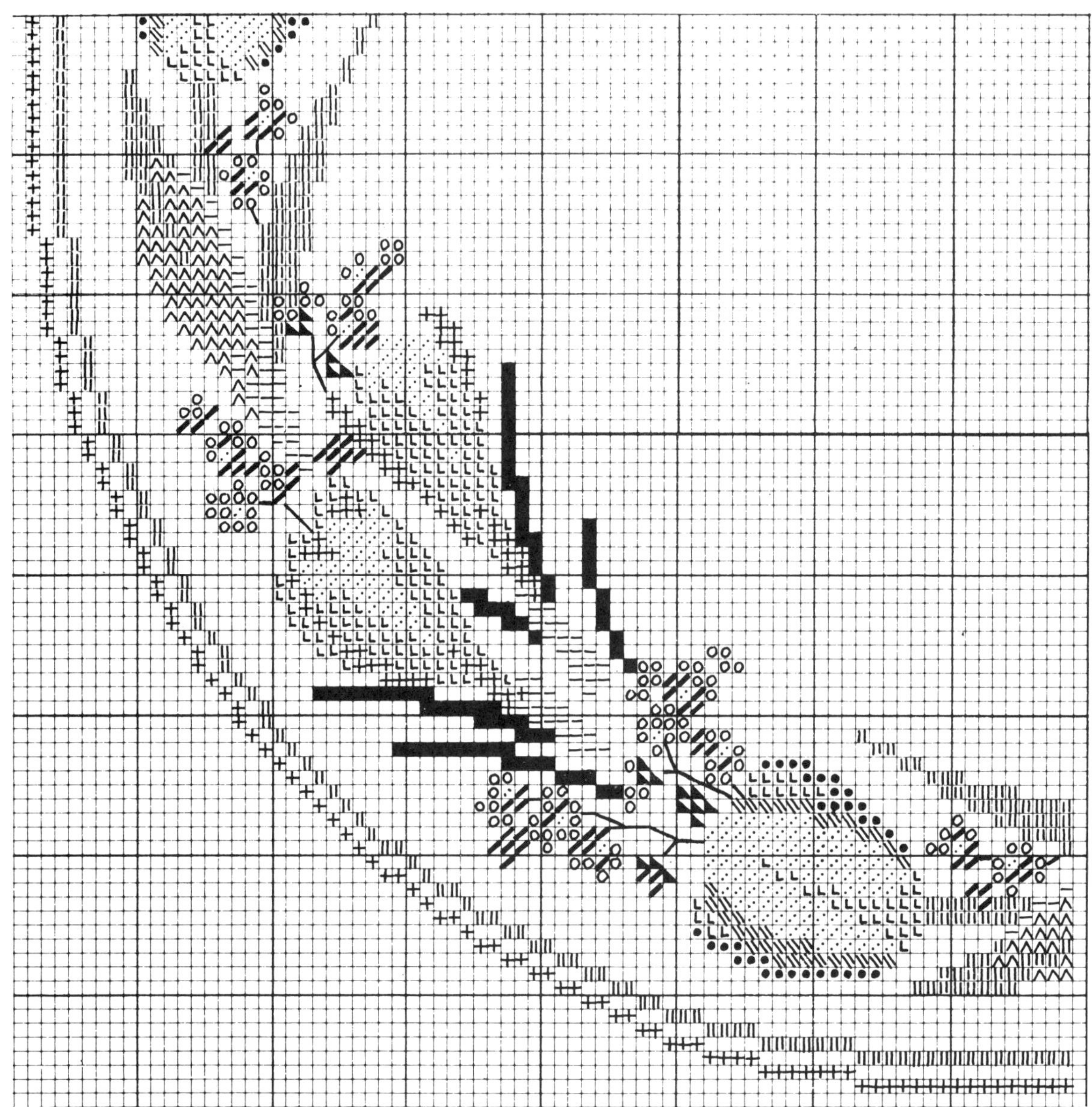

CIRCULAR DESIGN WITH TULIPS

(See color illustration on inside front cover.)

DMC #		DMC #	
606	bright orange red	793	medium cornflower blue
608	bright orange	794	light cornflower blue
741	medium tangerine	987	dark forest green
972	deep canary	3347	medium yellow green
444	dark lemon	471	very light avocado green
208	very dark lavender	3348	light yellow green

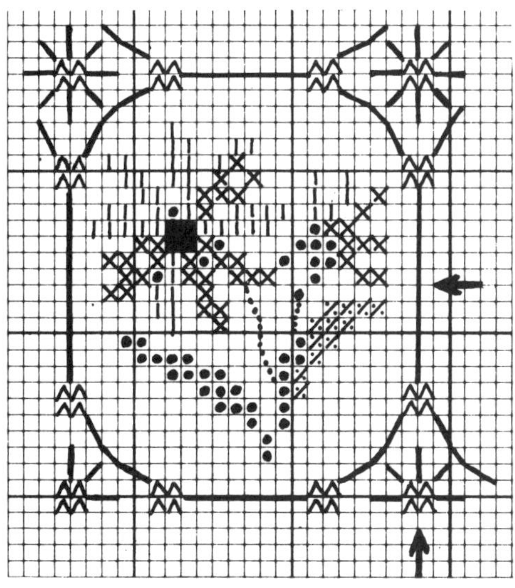

OVERALL PATTERN WITH OXEYE DAISIES

(See color illustration on inside front cover.)

	DMC #	
■	433	medium brown
— △	729	medium old gold
☒	972	deep canary
◫	973	bright canary
···· ●	470	light avocado green
◩	471	very light avocado green

OVERALL PATTERN WITH ROSEBUDS

(See color illustration on inside front cover.)

	DMC #	
— △	729	medium old gold
···· ■	987	dark forest green
☒	3347	medium yellow green
●	326	very deep rose
◫	961	dark dusty rose

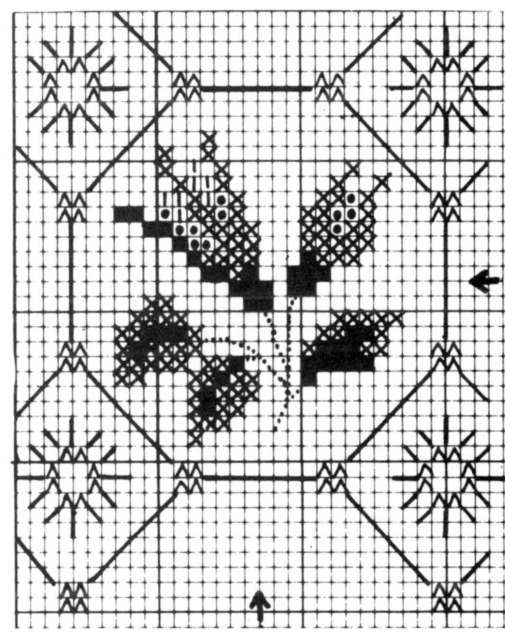

WALL HANGING WITH HOLLYHOCKS

(See color illustration on inside back cover.)

		DMC #	
	◪	309	deep rose
	⧄	335	rose
	z	894	very light carnation
	c	776	medium pink
	·	818	baby pink
	V	353	peach flesh
1 +	●	986	very dark forest green
2 +	☒	988	medium forest green
3 +	⫽	906	medium parrot green
4 +	⁒	907	light parrot green
	⁖	3348	light yellow green
	⌀	783	Christmas gold
	—	726	light topaz

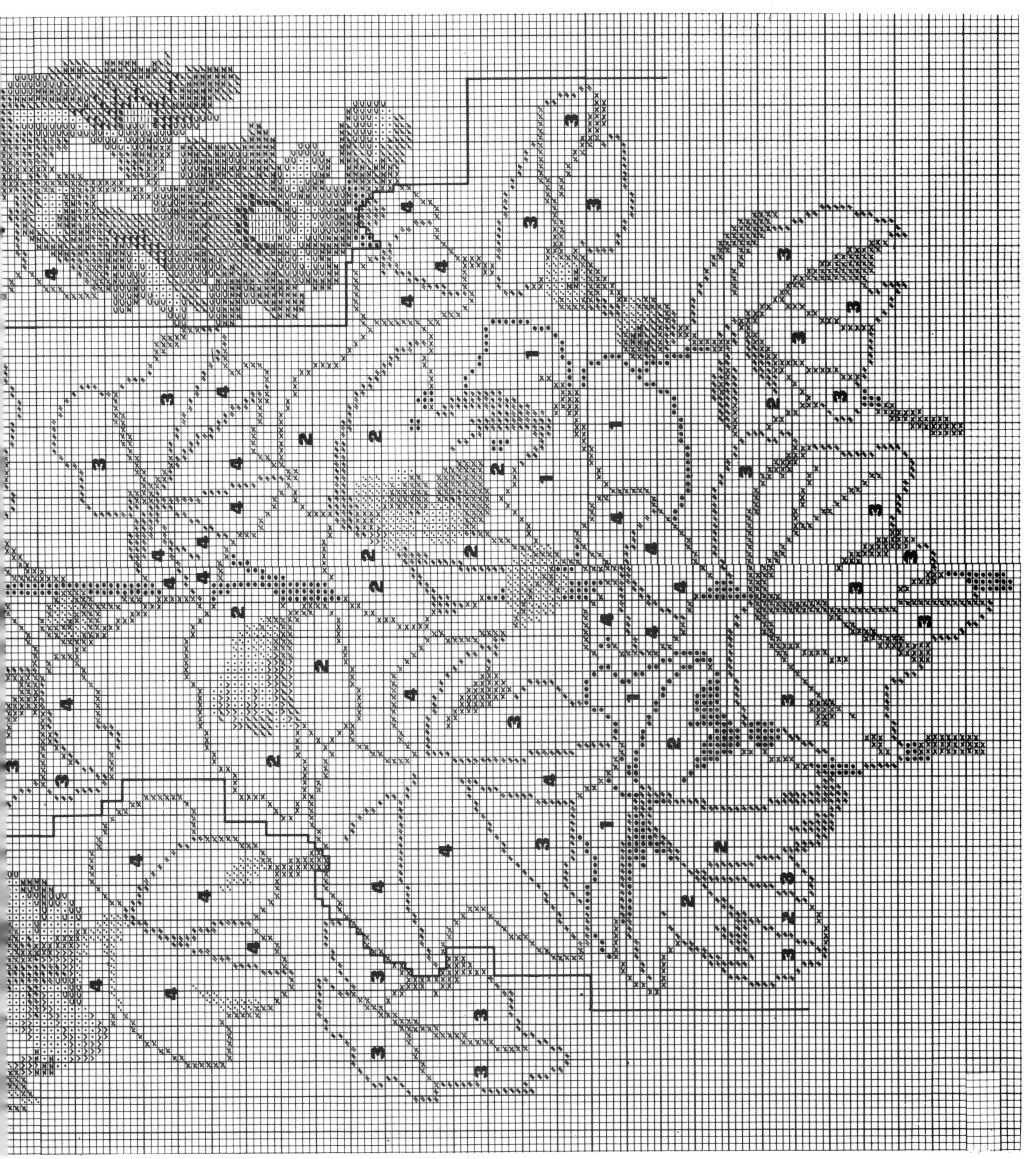

VERTICAL BORDER DESIGN WITH THISTLES, CLOVERS AND ROSES

(See color illustration on inside front cover.)

	DMC #	
◸	368	light pistachio green
N	320	medium pistachio green
◭	367	dark pistachio green
●	935	dark avocado green
↗	553	medium violet
ꓘ	550	very dark violet
C	3354	light dusty rose
◸	3350	very dark dusty rose
•		white
∴	973	bright canary
▼	729	medium old gold
—	733	medium olive green
V	502	blue green
6	501	dark blue green

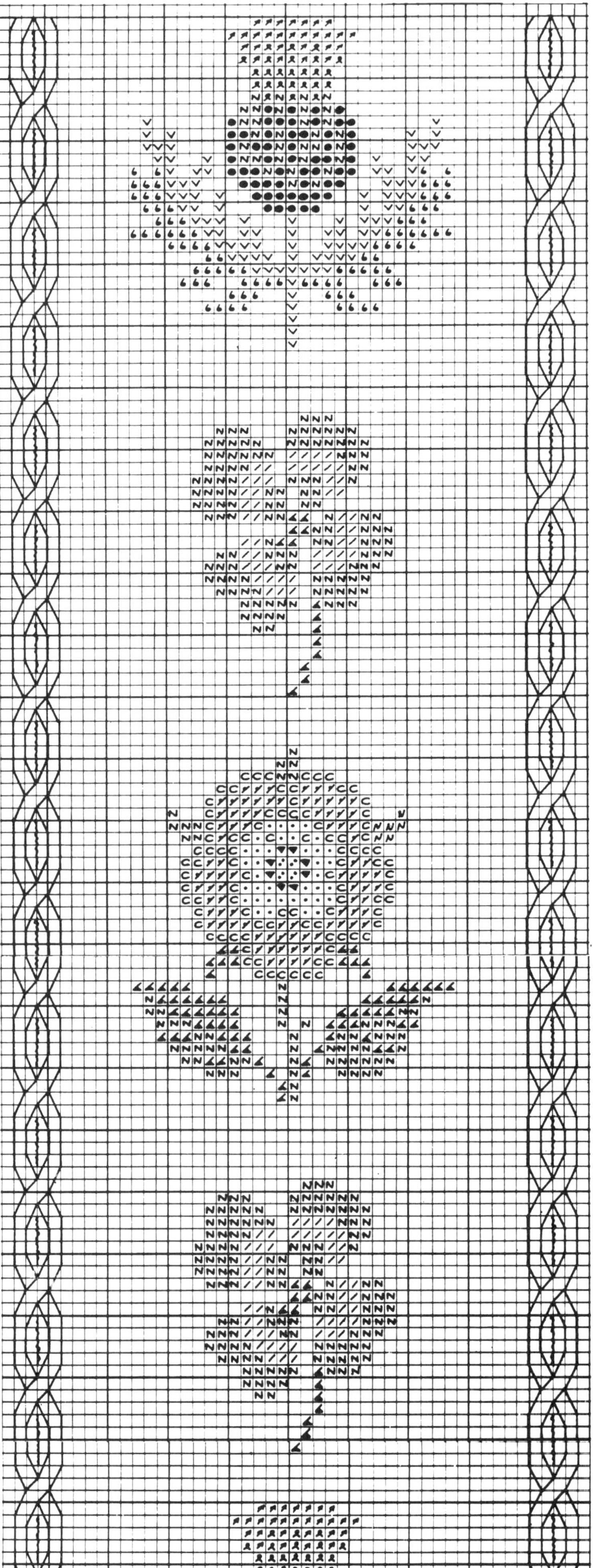

ROSE-BLOSSOM CUSHION DESIGN

(See color illustration on back cover.)

	DMC #				
■	937	medium avocado green	●	335	rose
◩	580	dark moss green	⊞	760	salmon
Ⅲ	581	moss green	⧅	761	light salmon
O	471	very light avocado green	⊡	754	light peach flesh
S	3012	medium khaki green	⊠	648	light beaver gray
◣	309	deep rose			

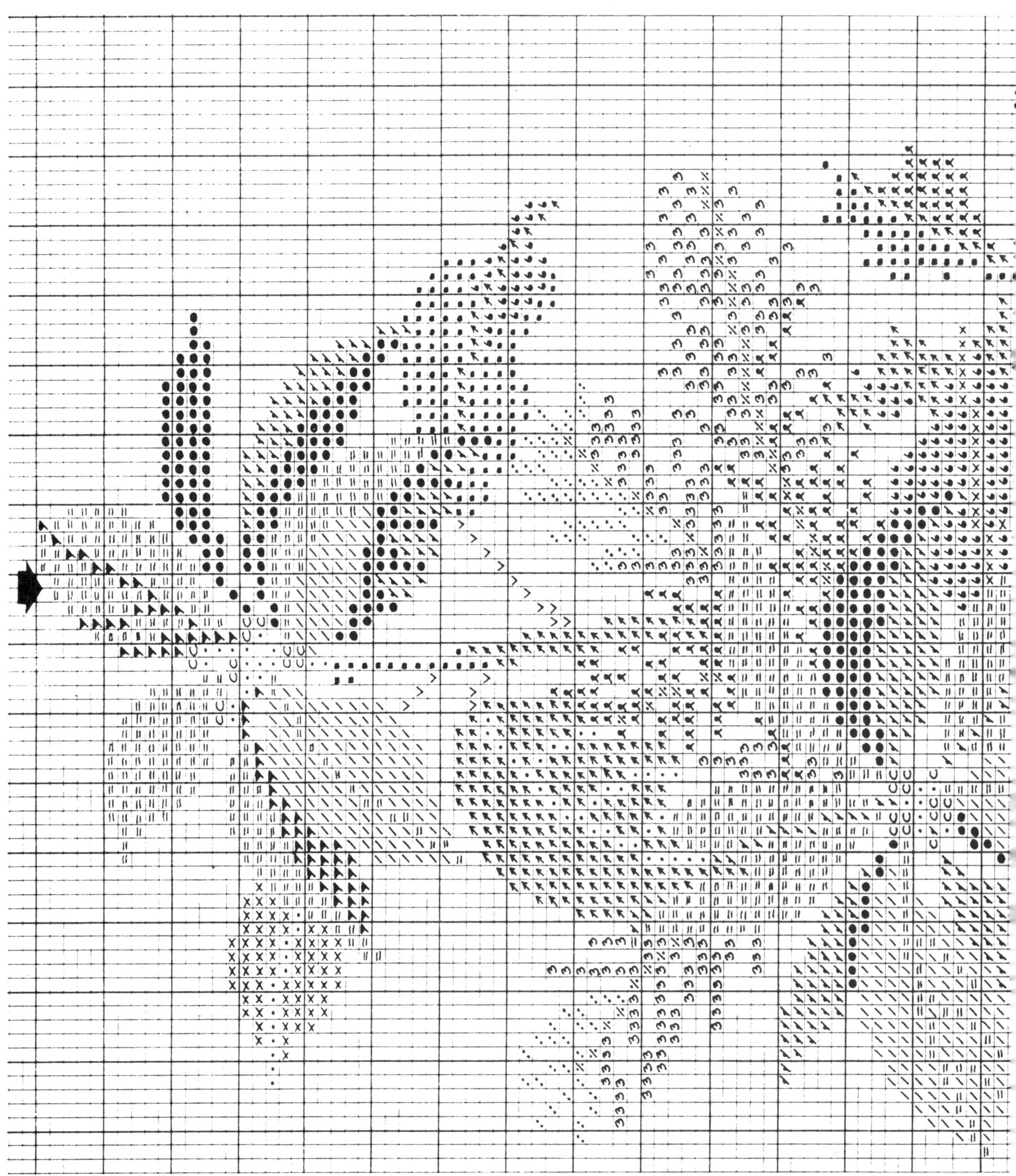

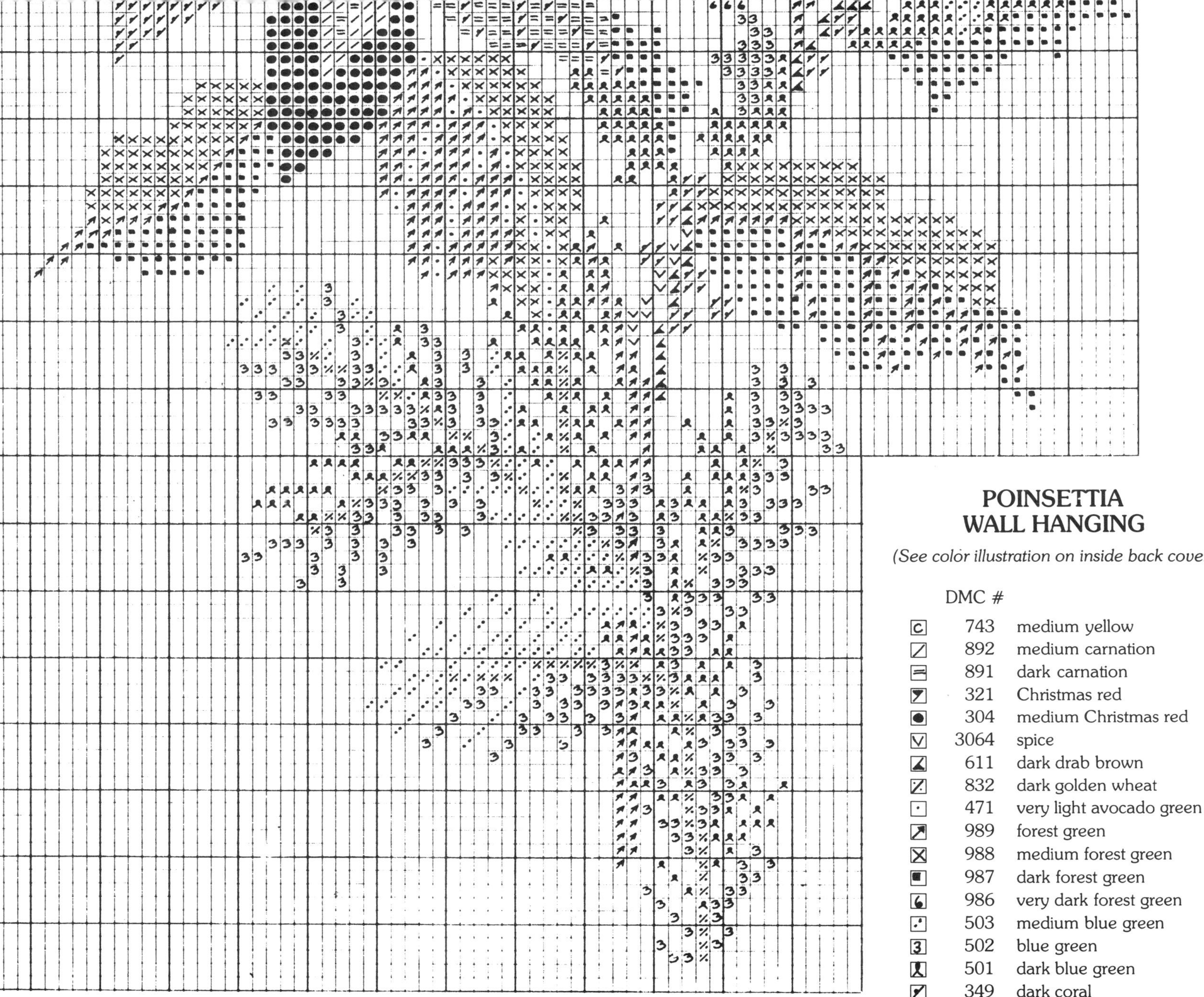

POINSETTIA WALL HANGING

(See color illustration on inside back cover.)

	DMC #	
C	743	medium yellow
/	892	medium carnation
=	891	dark carnation
◤	321	Christmas red
●	304	medium Christmas red
V	3064	spice
◢	611	dark drab brown
⁄.	832	dark golden wheat
·	471	very light avocado green
↗	989	forest green
X	988	medium forest green
■	987	dark forest green
6	986	very dark forest green
∴	503	medium blue green
3	502	blue green
♀	501	dark blue green
◤	349	dark coral

ALPINE-ROSE CUSHION DESIGN

(See color illustration on inside front cover.)

	DMC #			DMC #	
●	891	dark carnation	◢	3346	hunter green
↗	892	medium carnation	Z	3347	medium yellow green
Y	893	light carnation	/	3348	light yellow green
C	894	very light carnation	X	733	medium olive green
Ø	783	Christmas gold	IIII	927	medium gray blue
6	869	very dark hazel nut brown			

GENTIAN CUSHION DESIGN

(See color illustration on inside front cover.)

Symbol	DMC #	Color	Symbol	DMC #	Color
⁄.	809	delft	⫽	605	bright orange red
⁄	799	medium delft	— V	734	light olive green
⁄V	798	dark delft	↗	471	very light avocado green
6	796	dark royal blue	~~~ X	3347	medium yellow green
•		white	◢	3346	hunter green
C	818	baby pink			

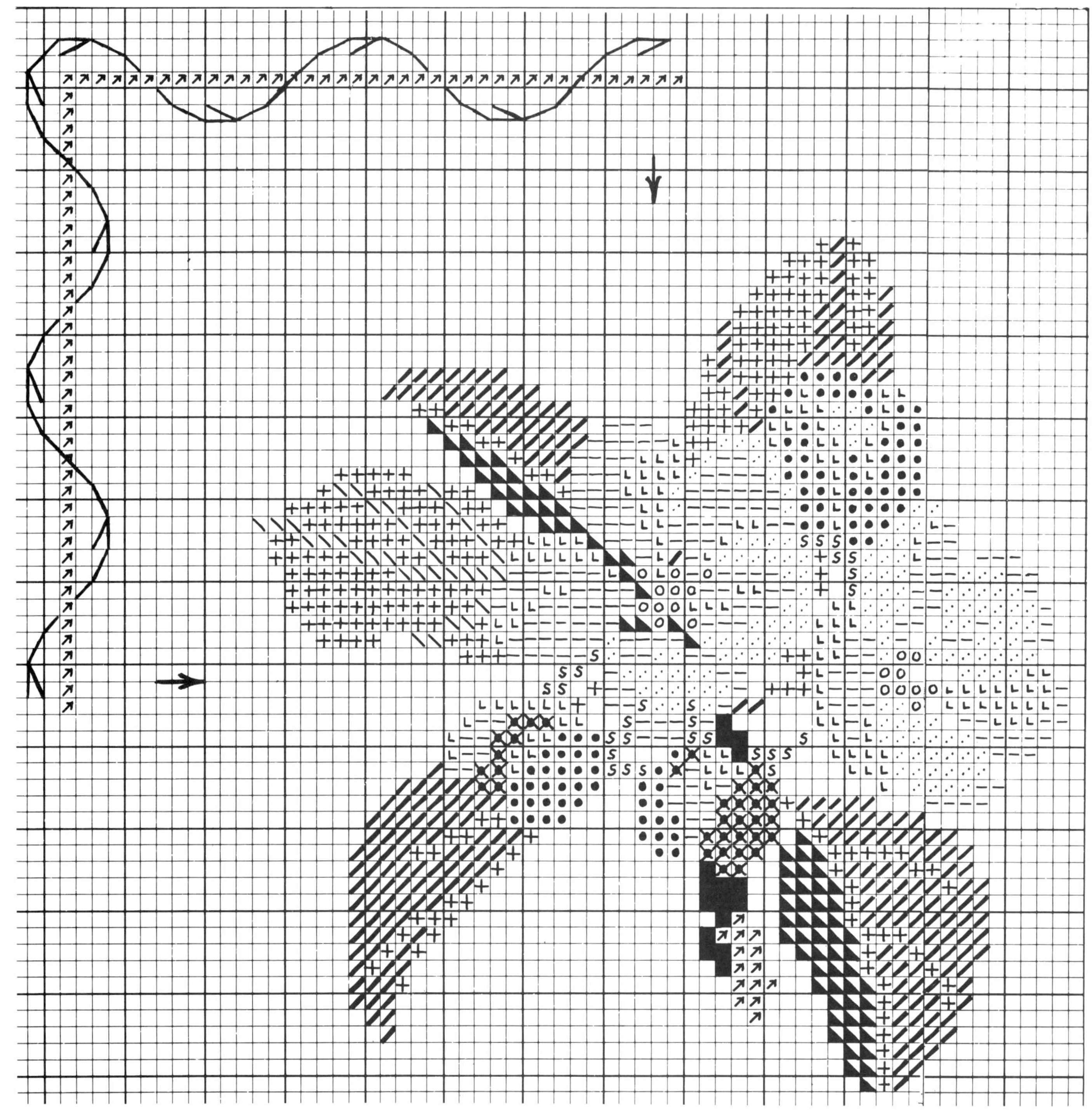

TWO APPLE-BLOSSOM DESIGNS

(See color illustration on inside back cover.)

	DMC #			DMC #			DMC #	
◣	3345	dark hunter green	O	725	topaz	L	776	medium pink
◢	3346	hunter green	■	610	very dark drab brown	—	818	baby pink
+	470	light avocado green	↗	612	medium drab brown	·		white
＼	3348	light yellow green	Ø	335	rose			
S	734	light olive green	●	899	medium rose			

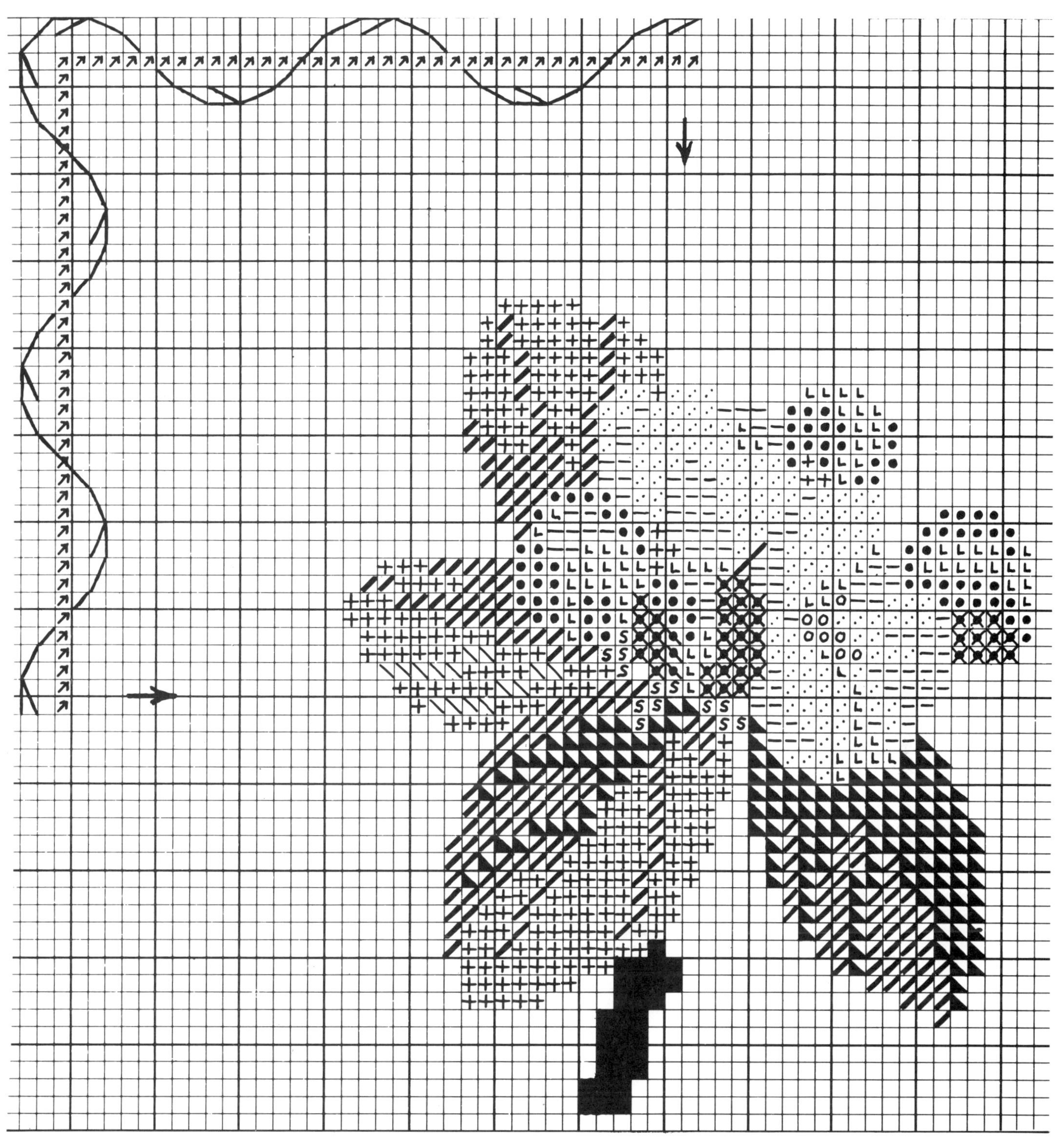

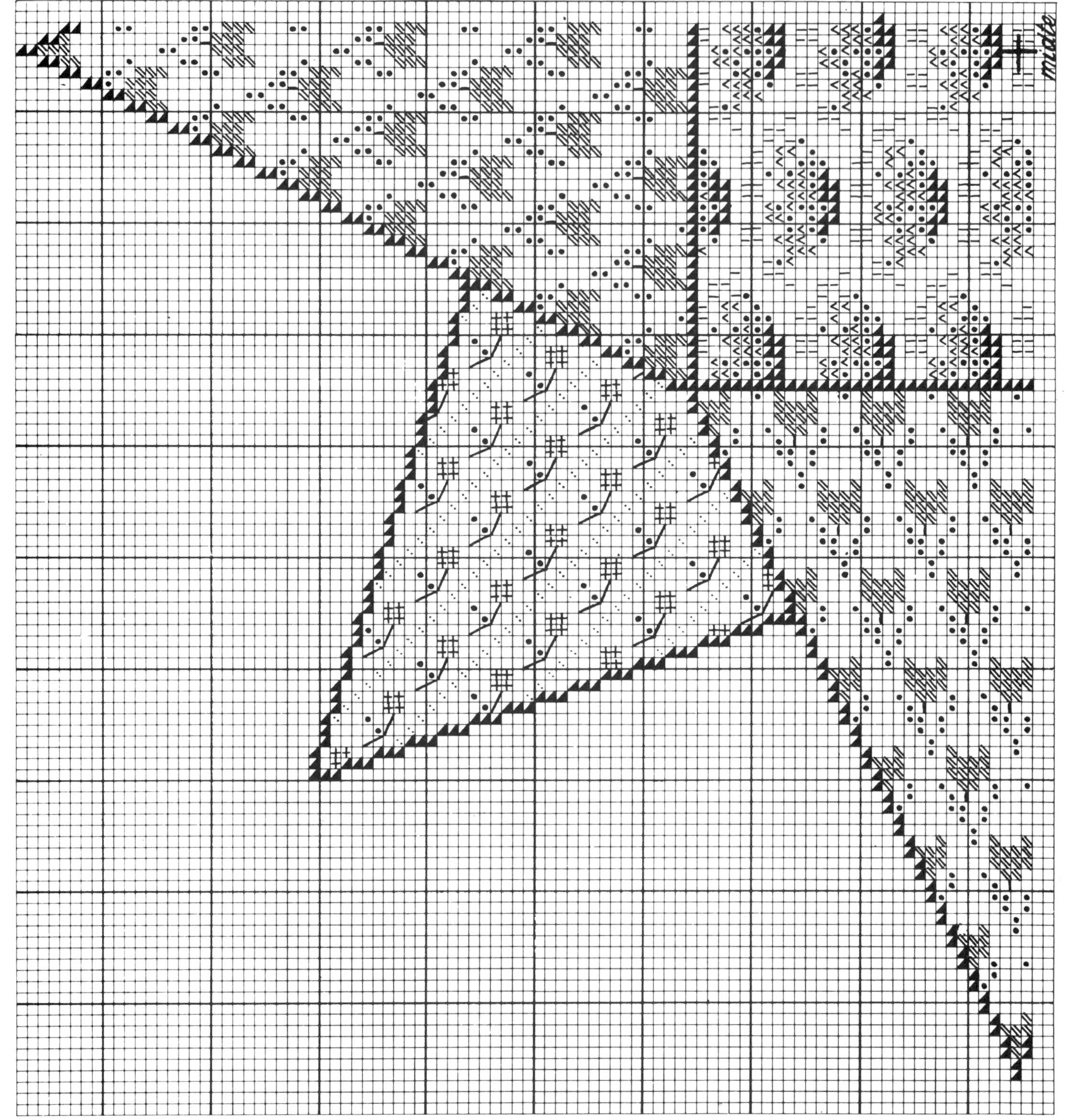

FLORAL PATCHWORK CHAIR COVER

(See color illustration on inside front cover.)

Symbol	DMC #		Symbol	DMC #	
◪	640	very dark beige gray	⊟	799	medium delft
—●	3347	medium yellow green	⁘	783	Christmas gold
⊞	899	medium rose	⧅	553	medium violet
<	798	dark delft			

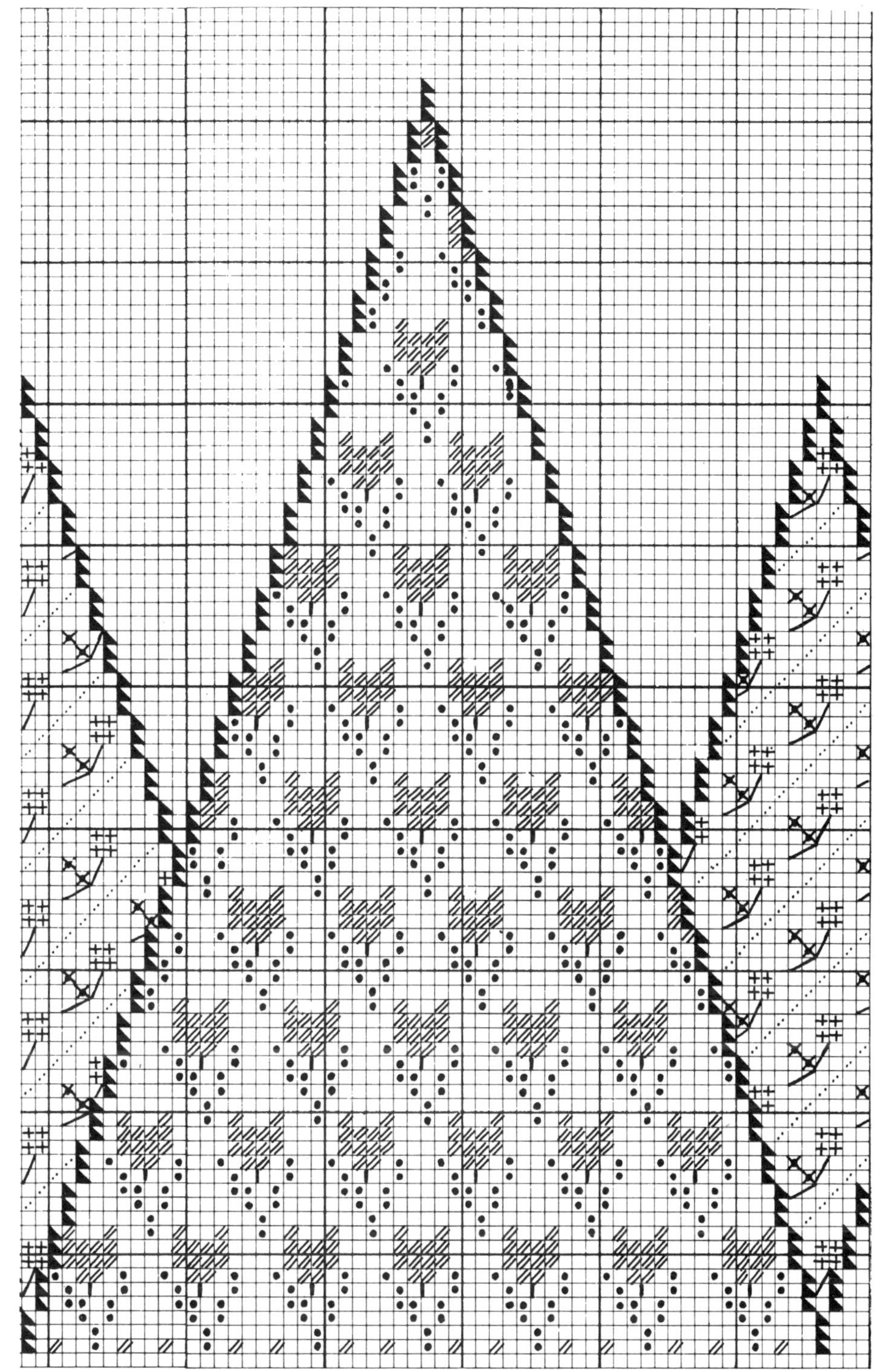

FLORAL PATCHWORK BORDER DESIGN

(See color illustration on inside back cover.)

DMC #		DMC #	
640	very dark beige gray	783	Christmas gold
3347	medium yellow green	553	medium violet
907	light parrot green	899	medium rose

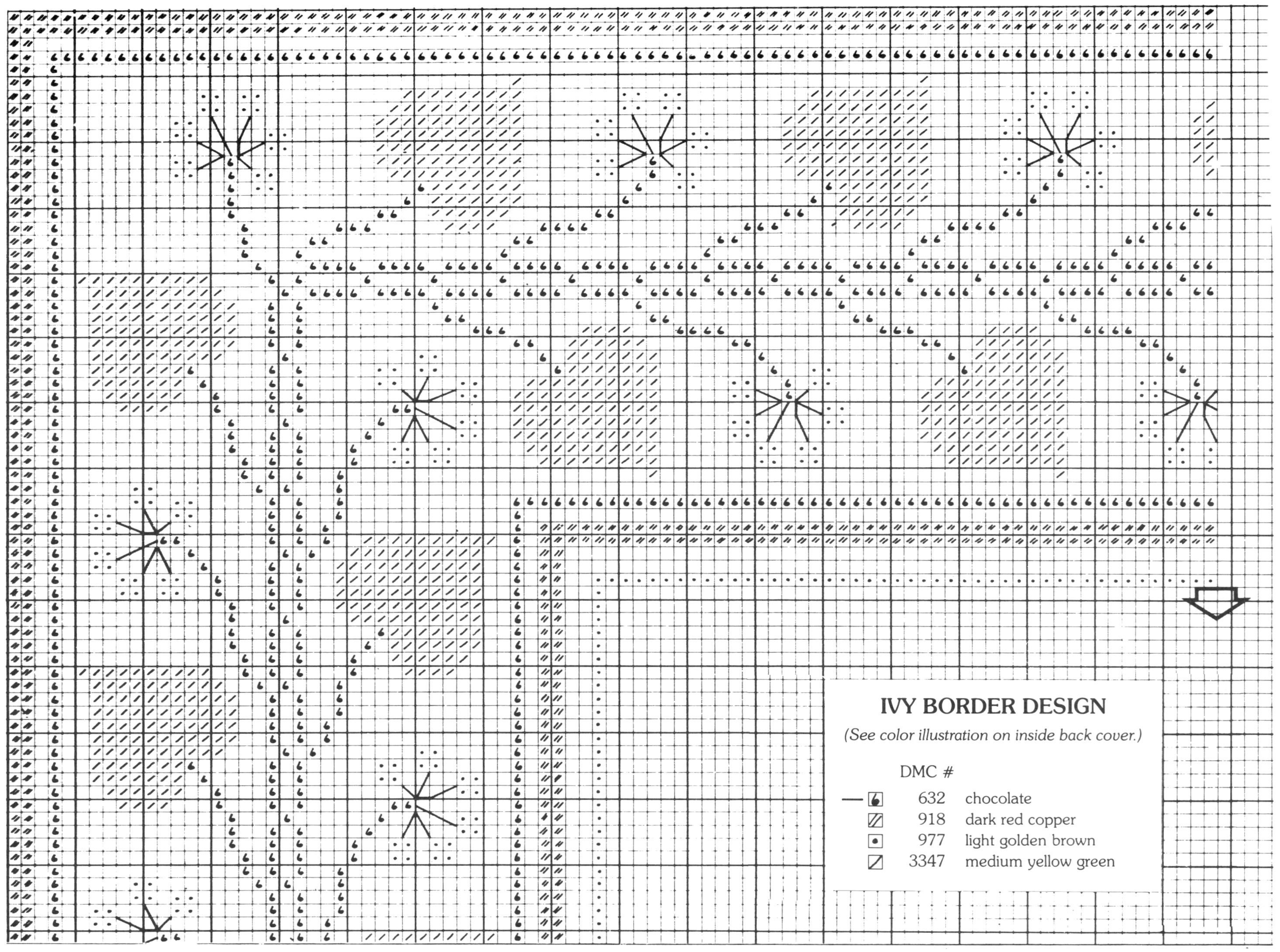

IVY BORDER DESIGN

(See color illustration on inside back cover.)

	DMC #	
— (symbol)	632	chocolate
(symbol)	918	dark red copper
(symbol)	977	light golden brown
(symbol)	3347	medium yellow green

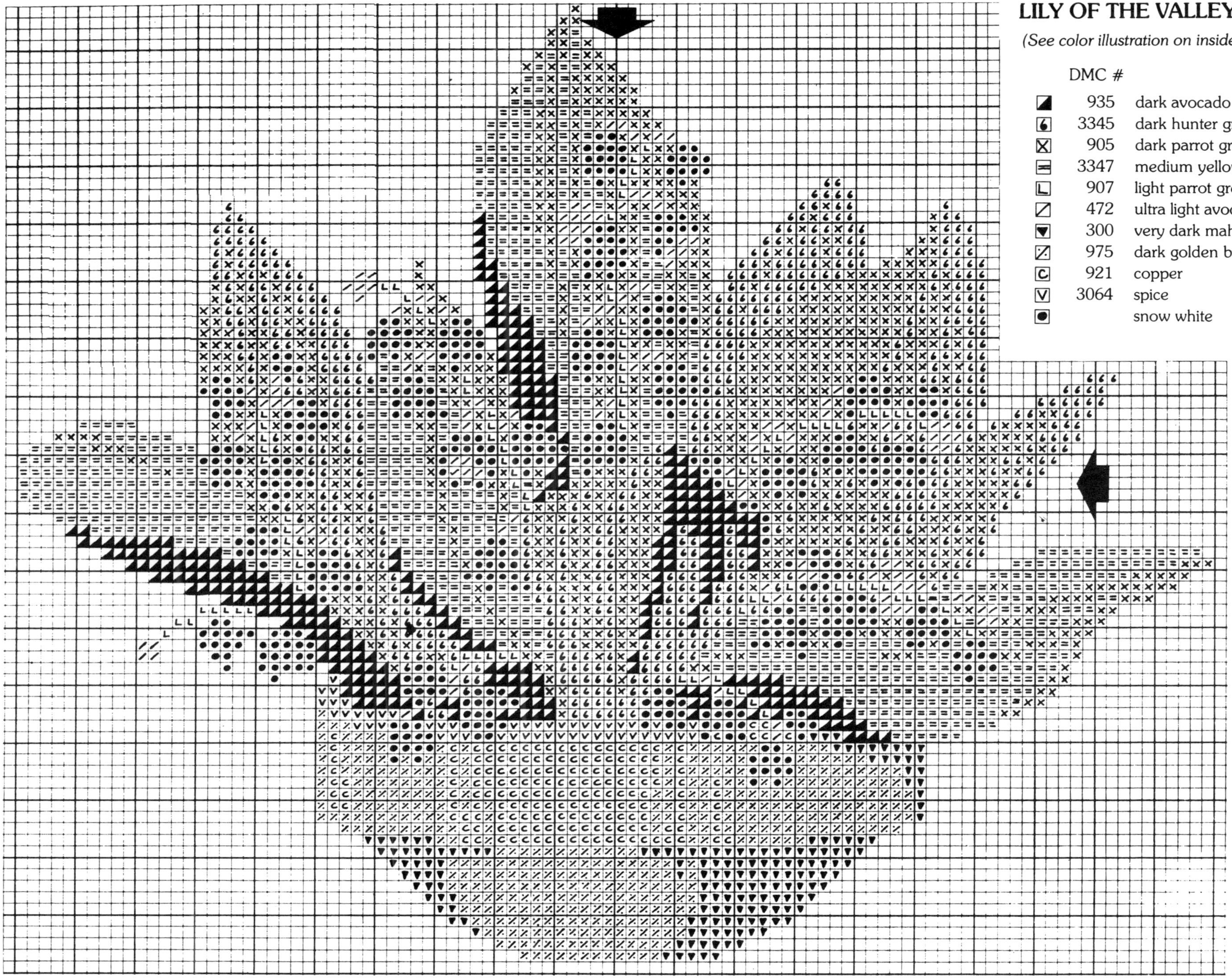

LILY OF THE VALLEY DESIGN

(See color illustration on inside back cover.)

Symbol	DMC #	Color
◢	935	dark avocado green
6	3345	dark hunter green
X	905	dark parrot green
=	3347	medium yellow green
L	907	light parrot green
/	472	ultra light avocado green
▼	300	very dark mahogany
⁄.	975	dark golden brown
C	921	copper
V	3064	spice
●		snow white

BELLPULL WITH ROSES

(See color illustration on inside back cover.)

DMC #	
3345	dark hunter green
3346	hunter green
470	light avocado green
471	very light avocado green
3013	light khaki green
781	dark topaz
972	deep canary
831	light avocado leaf
833	medium golden wheat
816	garnet
326	very deep rose
309	deep rose
892	medium carnation
893	light carnation
603	cranberry
604	light cranberry
818	baby pink
	white

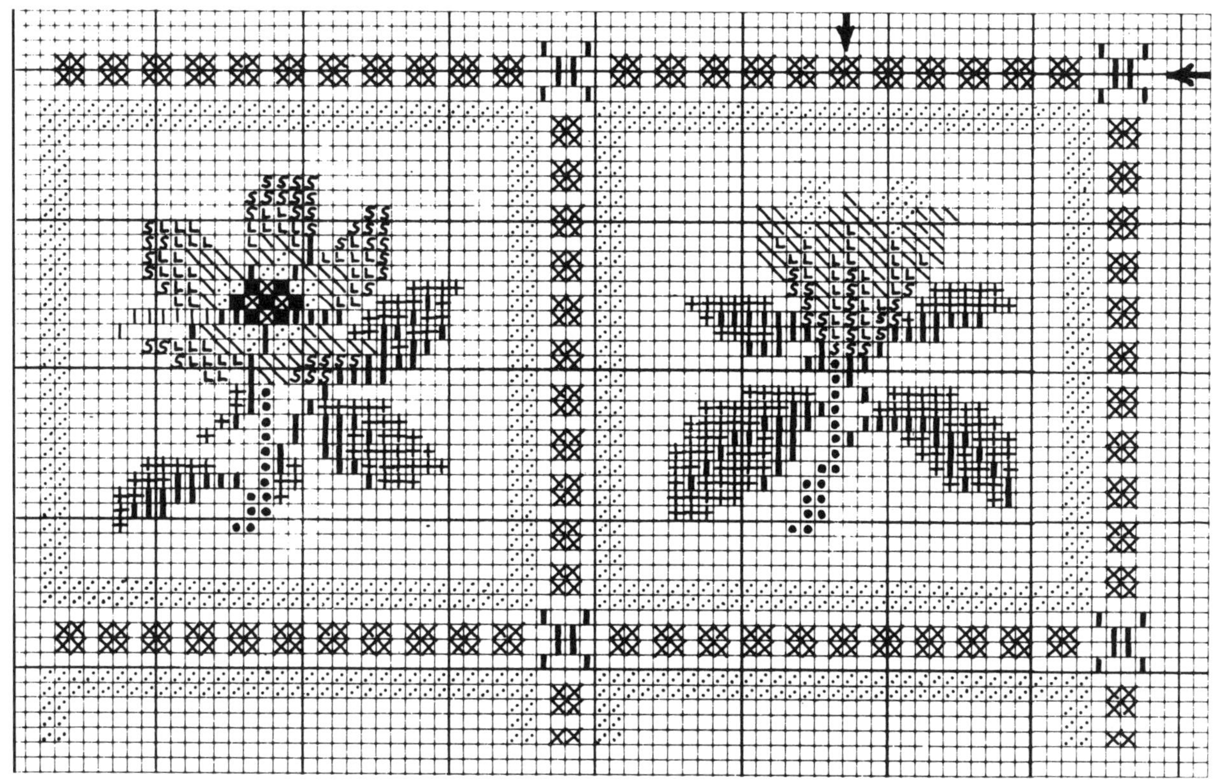

MAGNOLIA AND WILD-ROSE CUSHION DESIGN

(See color illustration on inside front cover.)

	DMC #			DMC #	
S	3688	medium mauve	⊠	726	light topaz
L	776	medium pink	●	612	medium drab brown
⧅	818	baby pink	I	471	very light avocado green
⁛	746	off white	⊞	472	ultra light avocado green
■	782	medium topaz			

WILD-ROSE BORDER DESIGN

(See color illustration on back cover.)

	DMC #	
■	3345	dark hunter green
●	580	dark moss green
⊠	581	moss green
I	471	very light avocado green
S	680	dark old gold
⊞	742	light tangerine
O	613	light drab brown
⊟	355	dark terra cotta
◣	891	dark carnation
◢	893	light carnation
L	894	very light carnation
⁛	754	light peach flesh

WALL HANGING WITH ROSES

(See color illustration on inside back cover.)

Symbol	DMC #	Color
●	895	dark Christmas green
6	3345	dark hunter green
☒	3346	hunter green
⁄.	470	light avocado green
V	471	very light avocado green
3	730	very dark olive green
⁄	3012	medium khaki green
◣	816	garnet
∅	304	medium Christmas red
ᴧ	891	dark carnation
═	893	light carnation
·	894	very light carnation

SIX STRAND EMBROIDERY COTTON (FLOSS) CONVERSION CHART

KEY: T = Possible Substitute * = Close Match — = No Match

DMC NO.	ROYAL MOULINÉ NO.	BATES/ ANCHOR NO.
White	1001	2
Ecru	8600	926
208	3335*	110*
209	3415*	105
210	3320*	104
211	3410	108*
221	2570	897*
223	2555	894
224	2545	893
225	2540	892
300	8330	352*
301	8315*	349*
304	2415*	47*
307	6005*	289*
309	2525*	42*
310	1002	403
311	4275T	149*
312	—	147*
315	3130	896*
316	3120	895*
317	1030*	400*
318	1020*	399*
319	5025	246*
320	5015	216*
321	2415	47
322	—	978*
326	2530*	59*
327	3365*	101*
333	—	119
334	4250T	145
335	2525T	42*
336	4270*	149*
340	—	118
341	—	117
347	2425*	13*
349	2400	13
350	2045T	11
351	2015T	11*
352	2015	10*
353	2010*	8*
355	8095	5968
356	8090	5975*
367	5020	216*
368	5005*	240*
369	5005	213*
370	—	889*
371	—	888*
372	—	887*
400	8325*	351
402	8305*	347*
407	8005	882*
413	1025*	401
414	1020*	400*
415	1015	398
420	8720*	375*
422	8710*	373*
433	8265	371*
434	8215	309
435	8210*	369*
436	8205	363*

DMC NO.	ROYAL MOULINÉ NO.	BATES/ ANCHOR NO.
437	8200*	362
444	6155*	291
445	6000	288
451	—	399*
452	—	399*
453	1015T	397*
469	5255	267*
470	5255*	267
471	5245	266*
472	5240	264*
498	2425T	20*
500	5125	879*
501	5120*	878
502	5110	876
503	5105	875
504	5100	213*
517	—	169*
518	4860*	168*
519	4855T	167*
520	—	862*
522	—	859*
523	—	859*
524	—	858*
535	1115T	401*
543	8500	933*
550	3380*	102*
552	3370*	101
553	3360	98
554	3355*	96*
561	—	212*
562	—	210*
563	—	208*
564	—	203*
580	5935	267*
581	5925	266*
597	4860*	168*
598	4855*	167*
600	2225*	59*
601	2225*	78*
602	2640*	77*
603	2720*	76*
604	2710	75*
605	2155	50*
606	7260	335
608	7255	333*
610	5825T	889*
611	5735T	898
612	8815*	832
613	5605*	956*
632	8530	936*
640	8625	903
642	8620*	392
644	8800	830
645	1115	905*
646	1115*	8581
647	1110	8581*
648	1100*	900
666	2405	46
676	6250	891
677	—	886*

DMC NO.	ROYAL MOULINÉ NO.	BATES/ ANCHOR NO.
680	6260*	901
699	5375	923*
700	5365*	229
701	5365*	227
702	5330	239
703	5320	238
704	5310*	256*
712	8600*	387*
718	3015*	88
720	—	326
721	—	324*
722	—	323*
725	6215	306*
726	6150*	295
727	6135	293
729	6255	890
730	—	924*
731	—	281*
732	5925T	281*
733	—	280*
734	—	279*
738	8245*	942
739	8240*	885*
740	7045	316
741	6125	304
742	6120	303
743	6210	297
744	6110*	301*
745	6105	300*
746	6100	386*
747	4850	158*
754	8075	778*
758	8080	868
760	2035	9*
761	2030	8*
762	1010*	397
772	—	264*
775	4600*	128*
776	2110*	24*
778	3110	968*
780	8215*	310*
781	8215	309*
782	6230	308
783	6220*	307
791	4165*	941*
792	4155T	940
793	4155	121
794	4145	120*
796	4340	133*
797	4265*	132*
798	4325	131*
799	4250*	130*
800	4310	128
801	8405	357*
806	4870T	169*
807	4860*	168*
809	4145*	130*
813	4610*	160*
814	2340T	44*
815	2530*	43

DMC NO.	ROYAL MOULINÉ NO.	BATES/ ANCHOR NO.
816	2530	44*
817	2415T	19
818	2505*	48
819	2000	892*
820	4345	134
822	8605*	387*
823	4400*	150
824	4225	164*
825	4215	162*
826	4210	161*
827	4605	159*
828	4850	158*
829	5825	906
830	5825*	889*
831	5825T	889*
832	5815	907
833	5815*	874*
834	5810*	874
838	8425*	380
839	8560	380*
840	8555	379*
841	8550	378*
842	8505	376*
844	1115T	401*
869	8720*	944*
890	5025*	879*
891	2135	35*
892	2130	28
893	2125*	27
894	2115T	26
895	5430*	246*
898	8425*	360
899	2515	27*
900	7230*	333
902	—	72*
904	5295*	258*
905	5295	258*
906	5285*	256*
907	5280*	255
909	5370	229*
910	5370*	228*
911	5465*	205*
912	5465	205
913	5460*	209
915	3030	89*
917	3020*	89*
918	8330*	341*
919	8095*	341*
920	8060*	339*
921	8060T	349*
922	8315T	324*
924	4830T	851*
926	4820*	779*
927	4810T	849*
928	1010T	900*
930	4510	922*
931	4505	921*
932	4500	920*
934	5070T	862*
935	5225T	862*

DMC NO.	ROYAL MOULINÉ NO.	BATES/ ANCHOR NO.
936	5260T	269
937	5260	268
938	8430	381
939	4405	127
943	4935*	188*
945	8020*	347*
946	7230*	332*
947	7255*	330*
948	8070	778*
950	8020T	4146
951	8020T	366*
954	5455*	203*
955	5450	206*
956	2170*	40*
957	2160T	40*
958	—	187
959	—	186
961	2515*	76*
962	2515	76*
963	2505	49*
964	—	185
966	5150*	214*
970	7040	316*
971	7045	316*
972	6120*	298
973	6015	290
975	8365	355*
976	8355	308*
977	8350	307*
986	5430	246*
987	5020T	244*
988	5295T	243*
989	5405T	242*
991	5165T	189*
992	4925*	187*
993	4915*	186*
995	4710	410
996	4700	433
3011	5525T	845*
3012	5525*	844*
3013	5515	842*
3021	—	382*
3022	—	8581*
3023	—	8581*
3024	1100	900*
3031	—	905*
3032	8620T	903*
3033	8610*	388*
3041	3215*	871
3042	3205*	869
3045	6260T	373*
3046	5810	887*
3047	5805	886*
3051	5530T	846*
3052	5060*	859*
3053	5055*	859*
3064	8005*	914*
3072	4805*	397*
3078	6130	292*
3325	4200	159*

DMC NO.	ROYAL MOULINÉ NO.	BATES/ ANCHOR NO.
3326	2115*	25*
3328	2045	11*
3340	—	329
3341	—	328
3345	5025T	268*
3346	5220T	257*
3347	5210*	266*
3348	5270*	265
3350	2220	42*
3354	2210	74*
3362	—	862*
3363	—	861*
3364	—	843*
3371	8435	382
3607	—	87*
3608	—	86
3609	—	85
3685	2335	70*
3687	2325	69*
3688	2320	66*
3689	2310	49
3705	—	35*
3706	—	28*
3708	—	26*
48	9000*	1201*
51	9014	1220
52	9006	1208
53	—	—
57	9002	1203
61	9013T	1218*
62	9000T	1201*
67	—	1211*
69	—	1218*
75	9002	1206*
90	9012T	1217*
91	9008*	1211
92	9011T	1216*
93	9007*	1210*
94	9011*	1216
95	9006T	1208*
99	9005T	1207*
101	9009*	1213*
102	—	1208*
103	—	1210*
104	9012	1217
105	9013*	1218
106	9002T	1203*
107	9003	1204
108	9014*	1220*
111	—	1218*
112	9003T	1204*
113	9007*	1210*
114	9010	1215
115	9004	1206
121	9007	1210
122	9010T	1215*
123	—	1213*
124	9007T	1210*
125	9009	1213
126	9006*	1208*